First World War
and Army of Occupation
War Diary
France, Belgium and Germany

14 DIVISION
Divisional Troops
D Squadron Duke of Lancaster's Own Yeomanry
23 May 1915 - 31 May 1916

WO95/1886/1

The Naval & Military Press Ltd
www.nmarchive.com
Published in association with The National Archives

Published by

The Naval & Military Press Ltd

Unit 10 Ridgewood Industrial Park,

Uckfield, East Sussex,

TN22 5QE England

Tel: +44 (0) 1825 749494

www.naval-military-press.com

www.nmarchive.com

This diary has been reprinted in facsimile from the original. Any imperfections are inevitably reproduced and the quality may fall short of modern type and cartographic standards.

© **Crown Copyright**
Images reproduced by permission of The National Archives, London, England, 2015.

Contents

Document type	Place/Title	Date From	Date To
Heading	1886/1 'D' Squadron Duke Of Lancasters Own Yeomary 1915 May-1916 May		
Heading	14th Division 'D' Sqdn D.L.O. Yeomanry May 1915-May 1916		
Heading	14th Division "D" Squadron D. L. O. Y. Vol. I 23.5-30.6.15		
War Diary	Le Havre	23/05/1915	24/05/1915
War Diary	Hellebrouck	25/05/1915	26/05/1915
War Diary	Broxeele	27/05/1915	27/05/1915
War Diary	Steenvoorde	28/05/1915	29/05/1915
War Diary	Boeschepe	30/05/1915	06/06/1915
Heading	14 "D" Sq. D. L. O. Y. Vol. 9		
War Diary	Boeschepe	07/06/1915	08/06/1915
War Diary	Westoutre	09/06/1915	13/06/1915
War Diary	Hilhoek (1 Unite N. W)	14/06/1915	18/06/1915
War Diary	Poperinghe (2 Unites W)	19/06/1915	22/06/1915
War Diary	Poperinghe (1 1/2 Miles W)	23/06/1915	30/06/1915
Heading	14th Division "D" Squadron D. L. O. Y. Vol. II 1-31.7.15		
War Diary	Poperinghe (1 1/2 Unites W)	01/07/1915	25/07/1915
War Diary	Watou 1 1/2 Miles E	26/07/1915	31/07/1915
Heading	14th Division "D" Squadron D. L. O. Yes. Vol. III From 1-31.8.15		
War Diary	Watou (1 1/2 mile E)	01/08/1915	31/08/1915
Heading	14th Division "D" Squadron D. L. O. Y. Vol IV Sept. 15		
War Diary	Watou (1 1/2 mile E)	01/09/1915	30/09/1915
Heading	14th Division "D" Squadron D. L. O. Y. Vol 5 Oct 15		
War Diary	In The Field	01/10/1915	31/10/1915
Heading	14th Division "D" Squadron D.L.O.Y. Vol. 6 Nov 15		
War Diary	In The Field	01/11/1915	30/11/1915
Heading	14th Div. "D" Squadron D. L. O. Yeomanry Vol 7 Dec 5		
War Diary	In The Field	01/12/1915	31/12/1915
Miscellaneous	'D' Squadron D. L. O. Yeomanry. Nominal Roll.	20/12/1915	20/12/1915
Heading	14 "D" Sq D.L.O.Y. Vol 8 Jan 16		
War Diary	In The Field	01/01/1916	29/02/1916
Heading	14 "D" D.L.O. Yeo Vol 10		
War Diary	In The Field	01/03/1916	31/05/1916

18861

"D" Squadron Duke of
Lancaster's Own Yeomanry
1915 May – 1916 May

14TH DIVISION

'D' SQDN D.L.O. YEOMANRY

MAY 1915 - MAY 1916

4 3 COYS

151/58x/5

IIt. Division

"D" Squadron S.O.K.

Vol: II. 23.5. — 30.6.15.

nov '15
nov '16

"D" Squadron D.L.O.Y.
14 F Divisional Cavalry.

Army Form C. 2118.

7/15.

WAR DIARY
or
INTELLIGENCE SUMMARY.
(Erase heading not required.)

Instructions regarding War Diaries and Intelligence Summaries are contained in F. S. Regs., Part II. and the Staff Manual respectively. Title pages will be prepared in manuscript.

Place	Date	Hour	Summary of Events and Information	Remarks and references to Appendices
LE HAVRE	23/5/15	9 A.M.	disembarked and proceeded to Camp I. No 3081 Pte Gregory admitted to No 8 Stationary Hospital	
"	24/5/15	4 P.M.	entrained and left at 8 p.m.	
HELLEBROUCK	25/5/15		arrived St OMER 3 p.m., detrained and marched to HELLEBROUCK.	
"	26/5/15		Nil	
BROXEELE	27/5/15	12-15 P.M.	marched via WATTEN to BROXEELE.	
STEENVOORDE	28/5/15	8-15 A.M.	marched to STEENVOORDE.	
"	29/5/15		Nil	
BOESCHEPE	30/5/15	6 A.M.	marched to BOESCHEPE to be attached to 5th Div Cavalry.	
"	31/5/15	12-30 P.M.	found digging party, 5 officers and 80 men improving trenches at ZILLEBEKE	
"	1/6/15	7 A.M.	1 officer 4 N.C.O.s patrol to 13th Brigade H.Qrs. H.29a.	
"	"		1 officer 30 O.R. felling telephone poles S. of YSER canal.	
"	"	12-30 P.M.	1 officer 20 O.R. entrenching near ZILLEBEKE.	
"	2/6/15	7 A.M.	2 officers 30 O.R. felling telephone poles N. of YSER canal to 13 Brigade H. Qrs. 12-30 P.M. 2 officers 30 O.R. entrenching near ZILLEBEKE	
"	3/6/15		Nil King's birthday.	
"	4/6/15	12-30 P.M.	1 officer 24 O.R. making dug out 13 Brigade H.Qrs. 6-30 P.M. 2 officers 34 O.R. entrenching E. of ZILLEBEKE	
"	5/6/15	6-30 P.M.	2 officers 62 O.R. entrenching E. of ZILLEBEKE.	
"	6/6/15	12-30 P.M.	1 officer 24 O.R. making dug out at 13th Bde. H.Qrs. 6-30 P.M. 1 officer 24 O.R. entrenching E. of ZILLEBEKE	

14

"δ" Sp: Nov.
Vol: 9

Army Form C. 2118.

"D" Squadron D.L.O.Y.
14th Divisional Cavalry

Instructions regarding War Diaries and Intelligence Summaries are contained in F. S. Regs., Part II and the Staff Manual respectively. Title pages will be prepared in manuscript.

WAR DIARY
or
INTELLIGENCE SUMMARY.

(Erase heading not required.)

Place	Date	Hour	Summary of Events and Information	Remarks and references to Appendices
BOESCHEPE	7/6/15	6.30 P.M.	2 officers 59 O.R. entrenching E. of ZILLEBEKE. 1 man wounded (3740 Pte W.J. Hunt).	
"	8/6/15	12.30 P.M.	1 officer 23 O.R. making dug out at 13th Bde H.Qrs. 6.30 P.M. 1 officer 23 O.R. entrenching E. of ZILLEBEKE	
WESTOUTRE	9/6/15	3 P.M.	Marched to camp 1 mile N.E. of WESTOUTRE	
"	10/6/15		NIL	
"	11/6/15	6 P.M.	2 officers 49 O.R. entrenching E. of DICKEBUSCH	
"	12/6/15	7.30 A.M.	1 officer 20 O.R. to BAILEUL for demonstration of poisonous gases.	
"	13/6/15	12.15 P.M.	Church Parade. 6 P.M. 2 officers 79 O.R. to DICKEBUSCH for entrenching, but recalled my hearty more	
HILHOEK (1 mile N.W.)	14/6/15	7.45 A.M.	Marched to camp 1½ mile N. of HILHOEK, on road from CASSEL to POPERINGHE.	
"	15/6/15	10.30 A.M.	1 officer 20 R. to WAMERTINGHE for demonstration of poisonous gases.	
"	16/6/15		NIL	
"	17/6/15	6 A.M.	2 officers 64 O.R. sent to CAESTRE to draw 60 remounts for 1st Division	
"	18/6/15		2 N.C.Os & 8 men returned from M.M.P. adjt. to Divisional M.P. Duties	
POPERINGHE (2 miles W.)	19/6/15	9 A.M.	Moved camp about 1 mile to farm 1½ mile W. of POPERINGHE	
"	20/6/15		NIL	
"	21/6/15		NIL	
"	22/6/15	9 A.M.	Moved camp to farm 1½ mile W. of POPERINGHE. 9 P.M. 2 N.C.Os & 12 men sent to report at 4 P.M. at 11 P.M. near YPRES. Services not required.	

Army Form C. 2118.

A. Squadron D.L.O.Y.
4th Divisional Cavalry

WAR DIARY
or
INTELLIGENCE SUMMARY.
(Erase heading not required.)

Instructions regarding War Diaries and Intelligence Summaries are contained in F. S. Regs., Part II. and the Staff Manual respectively. Title pages will be prepared in manuscript.

Place	Date	Hour	Summary of Events and Information	Remarks and references to Appendices
POPERINGHE (1½ mile W)	23/June		Nil.	
"	24	11 A.M.	Moved camp to farm to mile W.	
"	25		Nil	
"	26		Nil	
"	27		Nil	
"	28		Nil	
"	29	4.45 AM	1 officer & 60 O.R. to YPRES to dig cable trench.	
"	30	5.30 AM	2 officers & 60 O.R. to YPRES to dig cable trench.	

F.C.N. Hunt Major
O.C. 14th Div. Cavalry

121/6300

14th/15th Division

Dn Shaura D.L.O.Y.
Vol. II 1 – 31.7.15.

"D" squadron D.L.O.Y.
14th Territorial Cavalry

Army Form C. 2118.

WAR DIARY
or
INTELLIGENCE SUMMARY.
(Erase heading not required.)

Instructions regarding War Diaries and Intelligence Summaries are contained in F.S. Regs., Part II. and the Staff Manual respectively. Title pages will be prepared in manuscript.

Place	Date	Hour	Summary of Events and Information	Remarks and references to Appendices
POPERINGHE (Huts W)	July 1st	6 P.M.	1 officer 48 O.R. to YPRES to dig cable trench	
"	2"	6.30 AM	2 officers 37 O.R. to GODEWAERSVELDE to Field 37 Rennouvh- L- Sir - H.Q. Ars.	
"	3"	4.15 P.M.	1 officer 20 O.R. clicker to 41st Inf Bde - as salvage park - trenches for 3 days, relieving Cyclist Co.	
"	4"		Nil	
"	5"	6 P.M.	1 officer 48 O.R. to YPRES, carrying party for timber	
"	6"		Nil	
"	7"	4.30 P.M.	1 officer 20 O.R. relieved salvage park of 3rd not. 1 offr going to trenches, sent stunning (admitted to hospital with crushed foot/an accident)	
"	8"		Nil	5.30 P.M. 1 officer 35 O.R. to YPRES to dig a cable trench
"	9"	7 P.M.	Salvage park, 17th not, relieved by Cyclist Co.	
"	10"		Nil	
"	11"	9-30 AM	Church parade	
"	12"		Nil	(bombarded, returned without working)
"	13"	5.30 P.M.	1 officer 40 O.R. to YPRES to make a supporting point behind front line trenches, were delayed	
"	14"		Nil	
"	15"	2.30 P.M.	1 officer 16 O.R. to GODEWAERSVELDE to hand 16 Rennouvh's like those to Siv M.Q. Ars.	
"	16		Nil	

Army Form C. 2118.

"D" Squadron D.L.O.Y.
14th Div. Cavalry

WAR DIARY
or
INTELLIGENCE SUMMARY.
(Erase heading not required.)

Instructions regarding War Diaries and Intelligence Summaries are contained in F. S. Regs., Part II. and the Staff Manual respectively. Title pages will be prepared in manuscript.

Place	Date	Hour	Summary of Events and Information	Remarks and references to Appendices
POPERINGHE (Huile w)	July 17		Nil	
"	18	9:30 AM	Church parade	
"	19		Nil	
"	20		Nil	
"	21		Nil	
"	22	5:30 PM	2 officers, 5 O.R. to YPRES working on supporting trench	
"	23	4:30 PM	1 officer 30 O.R. relieved Salvage party of Cyclist Co.	
"	24		Nil	
"	25	5:30 PM	1 officer 45 O.R. to YPRES working on supporting trench	
WATOU 117 mile E	26	9 AM	Moved camp to 1 mile E. of WATOU on POPERINGHE road. Relieves Salvage Squad	
"	27	5:30 PM	1 officer 45 O.R. to YPRES working on supporting trench	
"	28		Nil	
"	29		Nil	
"	30	4:30 AM	Salvage Squad relieved by Cyclist Co.	
"	31	5 A.M.	1 officer 25 O.R. to GOEWAERVELDE to fetch & distribute 25 Reinforcements 6th Brigade	

121/6099

14th Squadron

"D" Squadron R.A.O. Yeo:
Vol: III
From 1 - 31. 8. 15

"D" Squadron D.L.O.Y.
14th Divisional Cavalry.

Army Form C. 2118.

WAR DIARY
or
INTELLIGENCE SUMMARY.
(Erase heading not required.)

Instructions regarding War Diaries and Intelligence Summaries are contained in F. S. Regs., Part II. and the Staff Manual respectively. Title pages will be prepared in manuscript.

Place	Date	Hour	Summary of Events and Information	Remarks and references to Appendices
WATOU (2 miles E)	August 1	9 A.M.	Church Parade	
"	2 "	3 P.M.	1 Officer 30 O.R. relieved Salvage Squad of Cyclist Co. 5.20 P.M. 1 Officer 23 O.R. to YPRES. Took on Castle Trench.	
"	3 "		Nil	
"	4 "		Nil	
"	5 "	7 A.M.	2 N.C.O's 19 O.R. to Police duty. 16th Div. H.Q.	
"	6 "	5.30 A.M.	Salvage party of 2nd relieved by 14th Cyclist Co. 2 men extra to Police duty	
"	7 "	5.45 P.M.	1 Officer 56 O.R. to YPRES. carrying party	
"	8 "		Nil	
"	9 "		Nil	
"	10 "	5.45 P.M.	1 N.C.O. 20 O.R. to YPRES working party	
"	11 "	5.30 P.M.	1 Officer 30 O.R. relieved Cyclist Co at Salvage.	
"	12 "	5.45 P.M.	1 N.C.O. 25 O.R. to YPRES. carrying party	
"	13 "		Nil	12. 2 men returned from Police duty.
"	14 "	5.45 P.M.	2 N.C.O's 25 O.R. to YPRES working party.	12.20 P.M.
"	15 "		Nil	
"	16 "	5.45 P.M.	2 N.C.O's 25 O.R. to YPRES working party. Salvage Squad relieved by Cyclist Co.	

D. Squadron D.L.O. Yeo.
14th Division

Army Form C. 2118.

WAR DIARY
or
INTELLIGENCE SUMMARY.
(Erase heading not required.)

Instructions regarding War Diaries and Intelligence Summaries are contained in F.S. Regs., Part II. and the Staff Manual respectively. Title pages will be prepared in manuscript.

Place	Date	Hour	Summary of Events and Information	Remarks and references to Appendices
WATOU (14 mile E)	17th		Nil	
"	18th	5.45pm	2 N.C.O's 25 men to YPRES working party. Two men wounded (Ptes Watson & Howard)	
"	19th	4.30pm	1 Officer 5 6.O.R. 2 N.C.O & 24 O.R. to YPRES working parties	
"	20th		Nil	
"	21st	6.30pm	1 Officer 4 O.O.R. 1 N.C.O. 20 O.R. to YPRES working party. 1 ly bus cancelled as men were full	
"	22nd		Nil	
"	23rd		Nil. 2nd Lieut H. Tatton joined us dead W. Heaton recalled.	
"	24th		Nil	
"	25th		Nil	
"	26th		Nil	
"	27th		Nil	
"	28th	4.30pm	1 Officer 4 7 O.R. 1 N.C.O & 180.O.R. to YPRES working parties. Horses shelled. Pte Richardson slightly wounded 2 horses killed.	
"	29th		Nil	
"	30th	5pm	1 Officer 57 O.R. to YPRES working party	
"	31st	2pm	2 Officers 30 O.R. to YPRES to relieve Cyclist to Salvage Squad.	

1899/121

14th Hussars

"D" Squadron D.O.R.
Vol IV
Sept. 15.

"D" Squadron D.L.O. Yeo.
14th Divisional Cavalry

Army Form C. 2118.

WAR DIARY
or
INTELLIGENCE SUMMARY.
(Erase heading not required.)

Instructions regarding War Diaries and Intelligence Summaries are contained in F.S. Regs. Part II. and the Staff Manual respectively. Title pages will be prepared in manuscript.

Place	Date	Hour	Summary of Events and Information	Remarks and references to Appendices
WATOU (Rémède)	Sept 1st	4 p.m.	1 officer 17 O.R. recalled from Salvage Squad, leaving 1 officer + 12 O.R.	
"	2nd		Nil	
"	3rd	2 p.m.	1 officer + 11 O.R. relieves Salvage Squad	
"	4th		Nil	
"	5th		Nil	
"	6th		1 N.C.O. + 24 men attached to 4th Cav. Bde. for timber felling. Salvage Squad relieved by Cyclist Co.	
"	7th		1 N.C.O. 35 O.R. working party to YPRES by train	
"	8th			
"	9th		Nil	
"	10th		Nil	
"	11th		Nil	
"	12th		Nil	
"	13th		Nil	
"	14th		48 O.R. working party under S.S.M. to YPRES by train. Pte Thornton wounded, rifle killed in leg	2 Lt Herbert Mayor O.C. 14th Div. Cavalry
"	15th		Nil	
"	16th		Nil	

D. Squadron S.I.O. 4ro.
.1st. Divisional Cavalry.

Army Form C. 2118.

WAR DIARY
or
INTELLIGENCE SUMMARY.
(Erase heading not required.)

Instructions regarding War Diaries and Intelligence Summaries are contained in F. S. Regs., Part II. and the Staff Manual respectively. Title pages will be prepared in manuscript.

Place	Date	Hour	Summary of Events and Information	Remarks and references to Appendices
WATOU 1½ mile E	Sept 17		NIL	
	18		NIL	
	19		NIL	
	20		1 Officer + 12 O.R. relieved Belot b. Cabage Squad.	
	21		Lt. & Guidon joined on appointment	
	22		NIL	
	23		1 Officer 25 O.R. working party	
	24	9.20	4 Officers 26 O.R. to trench. in Escort for prisoners to Cabage party relieved by Sgt Bolt 20	
	25		Escort for prisoners returned to Camp	
	26		Trench getting party returned from 4th Bn Dragoons	
	27		Cabage 1 Officer 30 O.R. relieved Belot B	
	28		NIL	
	29		NIL	
	30		NIL	

F.C.A. Hunt Major
O.C. 1st Div. Cavalry

121/7594

14th Kurram

"S" Squadron 5L.O.Y.
Vol 5
Oct 15

"D" Squadron D.L.O.Y.
14th Div: Cavalry

Army Form C. 2118.

WAR DIARY
or
INTELLIGENCE SUMMARY.
(Erase heading not required.)

Instructions regarding War Diaries and Intelligence Summaries are contained in F. S. Regs., Part II. and the Staff Manual respectively. Title pages will be prepared in manuscript.

Place	Date	Hour	Summary of Events and Information	Remarks and references to Appendices
Watou	July 1st		1 Officer 30 O.R. relieved Salvage Party	
	2		Nil	
	3		Nil	
	4		Salvage Party returned to Eecke	
	5		1 Sergeant + 10 men attached to Divl Hqrs for Police Duty	
	6		Nil	
	7		Nil	
	8		Nil	
	9		Nil	
	10		Nil	
	11		Nil	
	12		Nil	
	13		1 Officer + 21 O.R. for digging at 14th Divl Grenade School	
	14		do	
	15		do	
	16		Nil	

F. E. A. Hunt Major
O.C. 14th Div Cavalry

"D" Squadron D.L.O.Y.
14th Sin Cavalry

Army Form C. 2118.

WAR DIARY
or
INTELLIGENCE SUMMARY.
(Erase heading not required.)

Place	Date	Hour	Summary of Events and Information	Remarks and references to Appendices
	Oct 1915			
Sittingfield	17		Nil	
	18		1 Officer 20 O.R. for Salvage	
	19		Nil	
	20		Nil	
	21		2 Officers 50 O.R. to Poelbad for Remounts	
	22		Salvage Party returned	
	23		Nil	
	24		1 Officer reinforcement	
	25		Nil	
	26		Nil	
	27		1 Coyst + 10 Men returned from "Blue Duty"	
	28		Nil	
	29		Nil	
	30		Nil	
	31	8 A.M.	30 O.R. working party at 6th Corps R.E. Park.	

F. C. A. Hunt. Major
O.C. 14th Sin Cavalry

14th Hussein

B" Spasm stpr.
rot: 6
14/7624

Nov 15

K

"D" Squadron. D.I.O.Yeo.
14th Div: Cavalry.

Army Form C. 2118.

WAR DIARY
or
INTELLIGENCE SUMMARY.
(Erase heading not required.)

Place	Date	Hour	Summary of Events and Information	Remarks and references to Appendices
In the Field.	1		30 O.R. working party. 6 Corps. R.E. Park. 11 O.R. Carting Creeks for Stables.	
"	2		30 O.R. working party. 6 Corps. R.E. Park. 3 O.R. Carting hut Timber from R.E. Park.	
"	3		30 O.R. working party. 6 Corps. R.E. Park. 40 O.R. Carting hut timber from R.E. Park.	
"	4		30 O.R. working party. 6 Corps. R.E. Park. 7 O.R. Carting Creeks for Stables	
"	5		30 O.R. working party. 6 Corps. R.E. Park. 26 O.R. working party 15 "Div: Gunnery School.	
"	6		30 O.R. working party. 6 Corps. R.E. Park. "	
"	7		30 O.R. working party. 6 Corps. R.E. Park. 21 O.R. working party 15 "Div: Gunnery School.	
"	8		30 O.R. working party. 6 Corps. R.E. Park. 21 O.R. working "	
"	9		30 O.R. working party. 6 Corps. R.E. Park	
"	10		30 O.R. working party. 6 Corps R.E. Parks: 21 O.R. working party 14th Div: Grenade School	
"	11		30 O.R. " " " " 21 " " " "	
"	12		30 " " " " "	
"	13		30 " " " " "	
"	14		Nil	
"	15		Nil	
"	16		30 O.R. Working Party 6th Corps R.E. Park	

F. E. A. Hunt. Major
O.C. 14th D.I. Yeo Cavalry

Army Form C. 2118.

WAR DIARY
or
INTELLIGENCE SUMMARY
(Erase heading not required.)

Place	Date	Hour	Summary of Events and Information	Remarks and references to Appendices
In the Field	14th		30 OR Working Party 6th Corps R.E. Park.	
"	18th		" " " " " "	
"	19th		" " " " " "	
"	20		" " " " " "	
"	21		" " " " " "	
"	22		" " " " " "	
"	23		" " " " " "	
"	24		" " " " " "	
"	25		" " " " " "	
"	26		" " " " " "	
"	27		" " " " " "	
"	28		" " " " " "	
"	29		" " " " " "	
"	30		"	

F.C.A. Hurt Major
O.C. 14th Div. Cavalry

"Spain
St Lo. Lemans
vol 7

IX/7935

14th Feb

Dec 5

D Squadron - D.L.O. Yeomanry
14th Divisional Cavalry

Army Form C. 2118

WAR DIARY
or
INTELLIGENCE SUMMARY

(Erase heading not required.)

Place	Date	Hour	Summary of Events and Information	Remarks and references to Appendices
In the Field	Dec 1		30 O.R. Working Party 6th Corps R.E. Park	
"	2		" " " " " "	
"	3		Nil	
"	4		Nil	
"	5		Nil	
"	6		Nil	
"	7		39 O.R. Bringing Remounts from Cavalry Field Remount Depot	
"	8		Nil	
"	9		Nil	
"	10		Nil	
"	11		Nil	
"	12		Nil	
"	13		27 O.R. Bombing Class 14th Div. Grenade School	
"	14		" " " " "	
"	15		" " " " "	
"	16		Nil	
"	17		35 O.R. Bringing Remounts from Cavalry Field Remount Depot	
"	18			

F. E. A. Hunt Morgan
O.C. 1st Squ. Cavy

Army Form C. 2118

"B" Squn. D Zorl.
14th Div. Cav.

WAR DIARY
or
INTELLIGENCE SUMMARY
(Erase heading not required.)

Instructions regarding War Diaries and Intelligence Summaries are contained in F. S. Regs., Part II. and the Staff Manual respectively. Title Pages will be prepared in manuscript.

Place	Date	Hour	Summary of Events and Information	Remarks and references to Appendices
In the Field	Dec 19th		Nil	
	20		Nil	
	21		Nil	
	22		Nil	
	23		53 O.R. Bringing Remounts (Mules) from Field Remount Dept	
	24		Nil	
	25		Nil	
	26		Nil	
	27		Nil	
	28		Nil	
	29		Nil	
	30		Nil	
	31		Nil	

J. C. A. Hunt. Major
O.C. 14th Divnl. Cavalry

"D" Squadron. D.L.O. Yeomanry.
Nominal Roll.   20th Decr, 1915.

Officers.
Major F.C.A. Hurt.
Capt. J. Fitzherbert-Brockholes.
Lieut. J. Stanning.
  "   J.A. Grierson.
2nd Lt. P. Boddington.
  "   C. Gwyer.
  "   H. Tatton.

Other Ranks.

No.	Rank	Name	Remarks	No.	Rank	Name	Remarks
3427	S.S.M.	Scarisbrick R.W.		3742	Cpl. Saddler	Richardson J.R.	
3631	SQMS	Proctor H.A.					
3155	S.Farr Sgt.	Swift R.		2779	L.Cpl.	Waddington H.G.	
3370	Sgt.	Bowser G.		356	"	Furness J.	
3018	"	Morris F.		3565	"	Ogden J.	
3074	"	Harrison L.		3533	"	Evans W.	
3163	"	Ffoulkes C.H.		2600	"	Hodge J.A.	
3522	"	Thomas R.S.		2621	"	Hume G.	
3615	"	Macfarlane D.		3547	"	Cooper W.	
3173	"	Reed G.		3155	"	Jinks S.	
3031	"	Devin C.S.		2975	"	Parrington G.K.	
2436	L/Sgt.	Guy R.W.		2877	"	Cowell W.	
2873		Heller F.		3309	"	Fawcett F.	
3055	Cpl. S.S.	Howard J.		2996	S.S.	Dodd S.	
				3326	"	Hornby L.	
3246	Cpl.	Knowles F.H.		3328	"	Hogan G.	
3400	"	Pearson W.J.					
3529	"	Bird C.S.		3764	Tptr.	Bradshaw W.	
2521	"	Seed H.					
2382	"	Mueliner F.		3754	Pte.	Banks F.	
3585	"	Raynor F.		3911	"	Bannister	

No.	Rank	Name	Remarks	No.	Rank	Name	Remarks
3756	Pte	Benson. J.S.		3248	Pte	Hartley. C.	
3659	"	Beresford. H.		3901	"	Healey. H.	
3700	"	Blackburn. J.		3359	"	Hogg. D.	
4158	"	Boyes. T.V.		2698	"	Holding. W.	
				3158	"	Holland. W.H.	
3960	"	Cadman. W.H.		3551	"	Hough. J.	
3540	"	Cathro. T.E.		3343	"	Howard. C.	
3532	"	Christian. J.H.		2667	"	Hoyle. J.	
3912	"	Critchlow. C.E.		3759	"	Hudson.	
3578	"	Cross. W.					
				3593	"	Ikin. H.	
3793	"	Daynall. A.					
3758	"	Dobie. H.		4069	"	Johnson. H.	
3582	"	Davie. G.J.					
2893	"	Dixon. C.		3807	"	Kane. R.	
3679	"	do Jn.		4134	"	Kent. W.	
				4112	"	Knowles. J.	
3642	"	Edwards. J.					
				3247	"	Law. J.	
3259	"	Firth. W.		4149	"	Lees. G.A.	
3567	"	Fowler. R.		3547	"	Lopez.	
3847	"	Fuller. G.T.					
				3477	"	Mallalieu. H.	
3646	"	Garde. J.O.		3817	"	Mason. M.	
3809	"	Glennon. H.		4146	"	MacNemigall. W.	
3081	"	Gregory. W.J.		3553	"	Munday. A.	
3549	"	Gregson. T.S.		3806	"	Murdock. B.	
3554	"	Grey. J. ~~Gregson~~					
				4125	"	Naylor. C.	
3735	"	Harden. J.J.					
3613	"	Hargreaves. A.E.		4129	"	Patterson. W.G.	

No	Rank	Name	Remarks	No	Rank	Name	Remarks
3653	Pte	Pemberton S.		3562	Pte	Tattersall J.	
3070	"	Penswick A.		3979	"	Taylor G.H.	
3696	"	Potter J.		3668	"	do W.	
3978	"	Proctor W.		3315	"	Toohill B.	
3422	"	Pugh H.		2889	"	Townley J.	
3502	"	Puzey S.		3729	"	Travis E.	
				3719	"	Townsend J.	
4065	"	Ramsbottom A.		3748	"	Trott E.A.	
3691	"	Rogerson H.		3718	"	Tudor N.	
3649	"	Rooney W.					
				3417	"	Wagner C.H.	
3690	"	Sanderson T.		3087	"	Walker W.N.	
3076	"	Schofield		4070	"	Warwick J.	
3130	"	Scollon J.		3685	"	Watkinson T.	
3931	"	Seaman J.		3831	"	Whitaker H.	
3182	"	Sinclair G.M.		3528	"	Whitham D.K.	
3784	"	Slim		3301	"	Wilcock W.J.	
3574	"	Smith A.		3437	"	Williams J.	
3889	"	do A.J.		3694	"	Wilson T.	
3198	"	do J.		3429	"	Winspear J.	
3757	"	Stirling G.		3789	"	Wolstenholme A.	
3113	"	Sumner A.		3335	"	Woodcock R.	
3370	"	Sykes A.J.					

R.A.M.C. attached.
SS 448 Ashton H.
235 Pte. Strahan S.

J.C.A. Hunt Major
O.C. 14th Div. Cavalry

Army Form C. 2118

WAR DIARY
or
INTELLIGENCE SUMMARY
(Erase heading not required.)

Instructions regarding War Diaries and Intelligence Summaries are contained in F. S. Regs., Part II. and the Staff Manual respectively. Title Pages will be prepared in manuscript.

Place	Date	Hour	Summary of Events and Information	Remarks and references to Appendices
In the Field	Jan 1st		Nil	
"	2nd		14 OR Police Patrols	
"	3rd		"	
"	4th		"	
"	5th		"	
"	6th		"	
"	7th		"	
"	8th		"	
"	9th		"	
"	10th		"	
"	11th		"	
"	12th		"	
"	13th		"	
"	14th		"	
"	15th		"	
"	16th		"	
"	17th		"	
"	18th		"	
"	19th		"	
"	20th		"	
"	21st		"	
"	22nd		"	
"	23rd		"	
"	24th		"	
"	25th		"	

WAR DIARY or INTELLIGENCE SUMMARY

Army Form C. 2118

Place	Date	Hour	Summary of Events and Information	Remarks and references to Appendices
In the Field	Jan 26		14 OR. Police Patrols	
"	" 27		" " "	
"	" 28		" " "	
"	" 29		" " "	
"	" 30		" " "	
"	" 31		" " "	

F. C. A. Hurd Major
O C 7th Dn Cavalry

Army Form C. 2118

WAR DIARY
or
INTELLIGENCE SUMMARY
(Erase heading not required.)

D.L.O. Germany
14th Divisional
Cavalry

Place	Date	Hour	Summary of Events and Information	Remarks and references to Appendices
In the Place	Feb: 1		14 OR Police Patrols	
	2		" " " "	
	3		" " " "	
	4		" " " "	
	5		" " " "	
	6		" " " " 40 OR Salvage work	
	7		" " " " " "	
	8		" " " " 12 OR " "	
	9		" " " " 12 " "	
	10		" " " " 9 " "	
	11		" " " "	
	12		"Left St. Sixte Arrived Esquelbecq	
	13		Nil	
	14		"	
	15		"	
	16		"	
	17		"	
	18		"	
	19		"	
	20		"	
	21		"	

Army Form C. 2118

WAR DIARY
or
INTELLIGENCE SUMMARY
(Erase heading not required.)

Place	Date	Hour	Summary of Events and Information	Remarks and references to Appendices
In the Field	Feb:	22nd	Left Eauvelbecq. Arrived Villers-Bocage	
		23	Nil	
		24	Left Villers-Bocage. Arrived Bretell	
		25	Left Bretell Arrived Grand Rullecourt	
		26	Nil	
		27	Nil	
		28	Left Grand Rullecourt arrived Fosseux	
		29	Nil	

F.C.A. Hurd Mayor
O.C. 14 Div. Cavalry

14

"D" DLOYOO

Vol 10

Army Form C. 2118

WAR DIARY
or
INTELLIGENCE SUMMARY

(Erase heading not required.)

2/1 O. Yeomanry (30)
14th Div¹ Cavalry

Instructions regarding War Diaries and Intelligence Summaries are contained in F. S. Regs., Part II. and the Staff Manual respectively. Title Pages will be prepared in manuscript.

Place	Date	Hour	Summary of Events and Information	Remarks and references to Appendices
In the Field	Mar 1		Nil	
	" 2		"	
	" 3		"	
	4		"	
	5		"	
	6		"	
	7		"	
	8		"	
	9		"	
	10		"	
	11		"	
	12		"	
	13		"	
	14		25 O.R. Coal Fatigue at Saulty	
	15		" " " " "	
	16		" " " " "	
	17		50 " " " " "	
	18		25 " " " " "	
	19		22 O.R. Fatigue at HAUTEVILLE	

Army Form C. 2118

F. Sqdn 19th Yeomanry 14th Pvs'l 31
WAR DIARY or INTELLIGENCE SUMMARY
Cavalry

Place	Date	Hour	Summary of Events and Information	Remarks and references to Appendices
In the Field	Mar 20	25 OR	Coal Fatigue at SAULTEY. 22 OR Fatigue at HAUTEVILLE	
	21	22 OR	" Fatigue at HAUTEVILLE	
	22	30 OR	Supplies at SAULTEY. 22 OR Fatigue at HAUTEVILLE	
	23	30 OR	" " "	
	24	56 OR	" " "	
	25	56 OR	" " "	
	26	19 OR	" " "	
	27	Nil		
	28	"		
	29	11 OR	Bringing Remounts from SAULTEY	
	30	Nil		
	31	1 Officer + 30 OR	proceeded to WAVANS for Cavalry Training	

F. C. A. Hunt Major
O.C. 14th Sn. Cavalry

Army Form C. 2118

WAR DIARY
or
INTELLIGENCE SUMMARY

(Erase heading not required.)

J. Logan H.Q. Company
XIV "D" DO LON Y Vol 11

Instructions regarding War Diaries and Intelligence Summaries are contained in F. S. Regs., Part II. and the Staff Manual respectively. Title Pages will be prepared in manuscript. 14th Div. L.A.

T.A. Hunt OC 14th Div. Cavalry Major

Place	Date	Hour	Summary of Events and Information	Remarks and references to Appendices
In the Field	April	1	1 Officer 29 O.R. Cavalry training WAVANS. 5 O.R. Observation Posts	
		2	" " " " " " " " " "	
		3	" " " " " " " " " "	
		4	" " " " " " " " " "	
		5	" " " " " " " " " "	
		6	" " " " " " " " " "	
		7	" " " " " " " " " "	
		8	1 Officer 20 O.R. Police Duties VI Corps	
		9	" " " " " " " " " "	
		10	" " " " " " " " " "	
		11	" " " " " " " " " "	
		12	" " " " " " " " " "	
		13	" " " " " " " " " "	
		14	" " " " " " " " " "	
		15	" " " " " " " " " "	
		16	" " " " " " " " " "	
		17	" " " " " " " " " "	
		18	" " " " " " " " " "	
		19	" " " " " " " " " "	
		20	" " " " " " " " " "	
		21	" " " " " " " " " "	
		22	" " " " " " " " " "	
		23	" " " " " " " " " "	
		24	" " " " " " " " " "	
		25	" " " " " " " " " "	
		26	" " " " " " " " " "	
		27	" " " " " " " " " "	
		28	" " " " " " " " " "	
		29	" " " " " " " " " "	
		30	" " " " " " " " " "	

Army Form C. 2118

D. Sqdn. D.L.O. Yeomanry
14th Div¹ Cavalry

D. D.O.L. £0
V. & 12

WAR DIARY
or
INTELLIGENCE SUMMARY
(Erase heading not required.)

Place	Date	Hour	Summary of Events and Information	Remarks and references to Appendices
In the field	May 1		1 Officer 29 O.R. Cavalry training at WAVESNES. 1 Officer 19 O.R. Police Duties. 6 O.R. observatory	Posts
"	2		" " " " " " " " " " " "	"
"	3		" " " " " " " " " " " "	"
"	4		" " " " " " " " " " " 21 " " " "	"
"	5		left Fosseux marched to Sars-Le-Bois " " " "	"
"	6		N° 16 G⁵ instructional course " " " "	"
"	7		" " " " " " " "	"
"	8		" " " " " " " "	"
"	9		" " " " " " " "	"
"	10		left Sars-Le-Bois arrived Doullens	
"	11		left Doullens arrived Beaucourt.	
"	12		H. 16 G⁵ instructional class	
"	13		" " " "	
"	14		Nil	
"	15		Squadron training	
"	16		" "	
"	17		1 Officer 28 O.R. Police Duties 34 " " Dis⁵	Squadron training
"	18		" " " " " " " " "	"Vedette" used

D. Sqdn. 1/1 D.Y.
3rd Corps Cavalry

WAR DIARY
or
INTELLIGENCE SUMMARY
(Erase heading not required.)

Army Form C. 2118

24

Instructions regarding War Diaries and Intelligence Summaries are contained in F.S. Regs., Part II. and the Staff Manual respectively. Title Pages will be prepared in manuscript.

Place	Date	Hour	Summary of Events and Information	Remarks and references to Appendices
In the field	May 19th		1 Officer 28 o.R. Police Duties 34th Div= 50 o.R. Squadron Training	
	" 20		" " " " " " " " "	
	" 21		" " " " " " " " "	
	" 22		" " " " " " " " "	
	" 23		" " " " " " " " "	
	" 24		" " " " " " " " "	
	" 25		" " " " " " " " " 1 Officer 50 o.R. unloading party FRESHENCOURT	
	" 26		" " " " " " " " " 50 o.R. Squadron Training	
	" 27		" " " " " " " " "	
	" 29		" " " " " " " " "	
	" 30		" " " " " " " " "	
	" 31st		" " " " " " " " "	

Wheaton
Lieut
for O.C. D Sqdn D.L.O.Y.

www.ingramcontent.com/pod-product-compliance
Lightning Source LLC
Chambersburg PA
CBHW081459160426
43193CB00013B/2532